Maclaren

by George Forbes

LangSyne
PUBLISHING
WRITING *to* REMEMBER

LangSyne

PUBLISHING

WRITING *to* REMEMBER

Vineyard Business Centre,
Pathhead, Midlothian EH37 5XP
Tel: 01875 321 203 Fax: 01875 321 233
E-mail: info@lang-syne.co.uk
www.langsyneshop.co.uk

Design by Dorothy Meikle
Printed by Montgomery Litho, Glasgow
© Lang Syne Publishers Ltd 2011

ISBN 978-1-85217-102-5

Maclaren

SEPT NAMES INCLUDE:
MacPatrick
MacPhater
Paterson
MacGrory
Lair
Lawrence
Lawrie
Lawson
Macfater
Macfeat

Maclaren

MOTTO:
Creag an Tuirc
('the Boar's Rock').

CREST:
Between Two Branches of Laurel
a Black Lion's Head
Bearing an Antique Gold Crown.

TERRITORY:
Balquhidder and Loch Earn
in west Perthshire.

Chapter one:

The origins of the clan system

by Rennie McOwan

The original Scottish clans of the Highlands and the great families of the Lowlands and Borders were gatherings of families, relatives, allies and neighbours for mutual protection against rivals or invaders.

Scotland experienced invasion from the Vikings, the Romans and English armies from the south. The Norman invasion of what is now England also had an influence on land-holding in Scotland. Some of these invaders stayed on and in time became 'Scottish'.

The word clan derives from the Gaelic language term 'clann', meaning children, and it was first used many centuries ago as communities were formed around tribal lands in glens and mountain fastnesses.

The format of clans changed over the centuries, but at its best the chief and his family held the land on behalf of all, like trustees, and the ordinary clansmen and women believed they had a blood relationship with the founder of their clan.

There were two way duties and obligations. An inadequate chief could be deposed and replaced by someone of greater ability.

Clan people had an immense pride in race. Their relationship with the chief was like adult children to a father and they had a real dignity.

The concept of clanship is very old and a more feudal notion of authority gradually crept in.

Pictland, for instance, was divided into seven principalities ruled by feudal leaders who were the strongest and most charismatic leaders of their particular groups.

By the sixth century the 'British' kingdoms of Strathclyde, Lothian and Celtic Dalriada (Argyll) had emerged and Scotland, as one nation, began to take shape in the time of King Kenneth MacAlpin.

Some chiefs claimed descent from

ancient kings which may not have been accurate in every case.

By the twelfth and thirteenth centuries the clans and families were more strongly brought under the central control of Scottish monarchs.

Lands were awarded and administered more and more under royal favour, yet the power of the area clan chiefs was still very great.

The long wars to ensure Scotland's independence against the expansionist ideas of English monarchs extended the influence of some clans and reduced the lands of others.

Those who supported Scotland's greatest king, Robert the Bruce, were awarded the territories of the families who had opposed his claim to the Scottish throne.

In the Scottish Borders country - the notorious Debatable Lands - the great families built up a ferocious reputation for providing warlike men accustomed to raiding into England and occasionally fighting one another.

Chiefs had the power to dispense justice

and to confiscate lands and clan warfare produced a society where martial virtues - courage, hardiness, tenacity - were greatly admired.

Gradually the relationship between the clans and the Crown became strained as Scottish monarchs became more orientated to life in the Lowlands and, on occasion, towards England.

The Highland clans spoke a different language, Gaelic, whereas the language of Lowland Scotland and the court was Scots and in more modern times, English.

Highlanders dressed differently, had different customs, and their wild mountain land sometimes seemed almost foreign to people living in the Lowlands.

It must be emphasised that Gaelic culture was very rich and story-telling, poetry, piping, the clarsach (harp) and other music all flourished and were greatly respected.

Highland culture was different from other parts of Scotland but it was not inferior or less sophisticated.

Central Government, whether in London

"The spirit of the clan means much to thousands of people"

or Edinburgh, sometimes saw the Gaelic clans as a challenge to their authority and some sent expeditions into the Highlands and west to crush the power of the Lords of the Isles.

Nevertheless, when the eighteenth century Jacobite Risings came along the cause of the Stuarts was mainly supported by Highland clans.

The word Jacobite comes from the Latin for James - Jacobus. The Jacobites wanted to restore the exiled Stuarts to the throne of Britain.

The monarchies of Scotland and England became one in 1603 when King James VI of Scotland (1st of England) gained the English throne after Queen Elizabeth died.

The Union of Parliaments of Scotland and England, the Treaty of Union, took place in 1707.

Some Highland clans, of course, and Lowland families opposed the Jacobites and supported the incoming Hanoverians.

After the Jacobite cause finally went down at Culloden in 1746 a kind of ethnic cleansing took place. The power of the chiefs was curtailed. Tartan and the pipes were banned in law.

Many emigrated, some because they wanted to, some because they were evicted by force. In addition, many Highlanders left for the cities of the south to seek work.

Many of the clan lands became home to sheep and deer shooting estates.

But the warlike traditions of the clans and the great Lowland and Border families lived on, with their descendants fighting bravely for freedom in two world wars.

Remember the men from whence you came, says the Gaelic proverb, and to that could be added the role of many heroic women.

The spirit of the clan, of having roots, whether Highland or Lowland, means much to thousands of people.

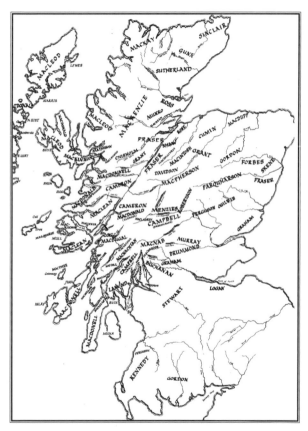

A map of the clans' homelands

Chapter two:

Lords of Balquhidder

The Clan Maclaurin, nowadays more commonly spelled MacLaren, was the name of a small tribal grouping belonging to west Perthshire and called in Gaelic the Clan Labhrin, this name being derived from the Gaelic name for the district of Lorn in Argyll.

As a result, the MacLarens bear the word 'Dalriada' - the old name for Argyll - above their coat of arms.

Romantic legend relates how the clan was descended from the seduction of warriors by mermaids, one of whom appears in their armorial bearings drawn up by the Lyon Court in the eighteenth century.

A more plausible yarn tells how one of the three sons of the Ulster King Fergus MacErc crossed over from Ireland and founded a fiefdom in Argyll in 503 which eventually stretched from Tiree into the central Highlands. It is from these

Irish colonists that the Maclaurins originally claimed descent.

The actual name Laurin may be a local dialect variation of Lawrence, a Christian martyr who suffered under the pagan Emperor Valerian's persecutions in 261 A.D.

A local Father Lawrence became Abbot of Achtow in Balquhidder in the thirteenth century and he was closely associated with the clan, being viewed as their unofficial 'padre'.

From the west coast the tribe of Laurin moved inland to Perthshire, having acquired from King Kenneth Macalpine, after his conquest of the Picts in the ninth century, the districts of Balquhidder and Strathearn.

Three brothers are recorded as having assigned to them in that territory the lands of Bruach, Auchleskin and Stank; and even in death, in the quaintly atmospheric Balquhidder kirkyard, which is celebrated for containing the graves of Rob Roy and his family, the burial places of the Laurin men are marked off in a special order so as to correspond with the topogra-

James Graham, the fifth Earl
and first Marquis of Montrose

phy of their estates and their corresponding rank in the clan.

The Maclaurins became followers of the mighty Celtic Earls of Strathearn and fought ferociously as allies in several major battles, including Bannockburn and, less successfully, at Sauchieburn in 1488 when King James III was defeated by rivals to his throne.

Maclaurins were also among those mown down by the billhooks of pikes and showers of arrows in the bloody mire of Flodden where their bodies were found near the slain king they had fought stalwartly to defend to the end.

They also fought for that tactical genius, the Marquis of Montrose, in his Royalist victories at Inverlochy, Auldearn, Alford and Kilsyth.

They also were in the forefront of the famous Highland charge that won the battle of Killiecrankie under the inspiring leadership of Claverhouse; and were consequently 'out' in all the succeeding Jacobite uprisings, eventually paying dearly - like so many other proud Highlanders - for their courageous loyalty to the lost Stuart cause.

In 1497, some of the clan of Laurin having carried off cattle from the Braes of Lochaber, the Macdonalds, the rightful owners of the cows, chased after the rustlers to get their herd back; and, overtaking them in Glenurchy, after a short, brutal fight recovered their four-footed goods.

The Maclaurins immediately sought the assistance of their kinsman, Dugal Stewart of Appin.

His mother was a Laurin and he was the illegitimate son of John Stewart, third Lord of Lorn. Some years previously the Maclaurins had been on his side when he tried vainly and illegally to seize his father's lands and 130 clansmen had fallen in a bloody battle that had taken place at the foot of Bendoran, a mountain peak in Glenurchy.

Dugal therefore was only too keen to help out the Maclaurins with his followers; and the Macdonalds were in turn hunted down. A savage fight took place at the Black Mount, near the head of Glencoe, during which Dugal was killed as was Macdonald of Keppoch, leader of his clan.

The battle proved indecisive and the cattle

that had been the root of the problem merely stampeded wildly into the heather clad hills as the slopes turned red with the blood of dead clansmen.

Balquhidder, by the picturesque shores of Loch Voil, became renowned as 'the country of the Maclaurins' which they were determined to hold by force of arms against all incomers.

So powerful were they in the area that nobody dared to enter the kirk until all the Maclaurins had taken their seats.

But even this seemingly peaceful tradition sometimes led to violence as there were unseemly brawls at the church door; and in 1532, the local minister himself, the Rev. John Maclaurin, was killed at the door and his murderers outlawed as a result.

Behind the kirk stood the rallying place of the clan known as Creag an Turic ('The Boar's Rock') which is a small hill overlooking the surrounding territory and approached by a steep path.

Thus 'Creag an Turic' became the clan's battle cry; and in 1987 the MacLaren Clan Society erected a cairn on top of this rallying point.

Clan warfare produced a society where courage and tenacity were greatly admired

Chapter three:

Lethal feuds

A deadly feud existed between the Maclaurins and the MacGregors since the latter were being persecuted by the Campbells around their traditional fiefdoms on the shores of Loch Lomond and were being unwillingly pushed into Perthshire.

The untamed MacGregors were notorious for pillaging and plundering; and in the sixteenth century they slaughtered 18 householders of their Maclaurin rivals and took possession of their farms. Even women and children were slaughtered.

It took another 46 years before these crimes were even investigated and the culprits brought to book: but a court intimidated by their kinsmen found the accused not guilty.

It needed Stewart of Appin two centuries later to regain the farms for the Maclaurins - and he could only do it at the head of 200 bloodthirsty and heavily armed warriors.

It did them little good in the long term because the properties were seized by the Crown after the '45 when the Maclaurins were condemned as rebels; and ironically in 1798 the farms were legally bought at a knockdown price by the chief of the MacGregors from the Commissioners of the Forfeited Estates.

In the '45 the Maclaurins followed the flags of the Murrays of Athole and the Stewarts of Appin. They fought throughout the campaign and savoured the sweet success of early victory and the bitter taste of final defeat.

Such was their notoriety that the Maclaurins were listed in government warrants as being 'among the most dangerous of West Highland clans'.

At Culloden they had fought bravely alongside the Appin regiment under Lord George Murray, brother of the Duke of Atholl, who in Gaelic urged them into one last futile but breathtakingly audacious charge which actually broke the Hanoverian line of redcoats before running out of momentum.

Donald MacLaren of Wester Invernentie was taken prisoner after Culloden, having watched a dozen of his kinsmen killed by musket fire.

He was being marched south to face trial and almost certain execution at Carlisle when the armed party made its way through the rocky defiles of the Lowther Hills above Moffat.

The prisoner, who had formerly driven his cattle southward to English markets by the same route and knew the terrain well, asked to relieve himself at the abyss which formed the vast natural grassy hollow known as the Devil's Beeftub where cattle rustlers were fond of hiding their ill-gotten gains.

Free for a fleeting moment from his escorts, he seized the opportunity by leaping over the edge of a cliff and plunging into a peaty bog many feet below where he promptly placed a turf on his head.

Eluding his pursuers until nightfall, he then returned back home to Balquhidder where he lived, disguised as a woman (he even had a few passing flirtations), until the Act of Indemnity set him free to reveal his true self.

This episode was later used by Sir Walter Scott in his novel *Redgauntlet*.

Another rival clan were the neighbouring Buchanans; and, in the mid-sixteenth century, a country fair took place at Kilmahog at the foot of the Pass of Leny where one of the young gallants from the Maclaurins of Balquidder was strolling along when he ran into a Buchanan who, in jest, lightly struck him across the face with the tail of a newly caught salmon he was carrying.

The young Maclaurin man went red in the face and then challenged his assailant to do the same thing with a fish's tail the following month at the Balquhidder fair.

The Buchanan youth apparently went home and totally forgot about the incident: but on the day of the Balquhidder gathering, as the Maclaurins were relaxing and enjoying them-selves buying, selling and taking part in vigorous sports, word suddenly arrived that a considerable body of Buchanans was marching up through

Strathyre and were already no further away than the nearby Clachan of Ruskachan.

It was during these tense moments that the affronted Maclaurin youth who had received the fishy slap in the face took it upon himself to loudly recall the insult.

The fiery cross was swiftly sent round the clan country and the Maclaurins rushed to arms, eager for a fight.

By the time the Buchanans had arrived on the scene, the Balquhidder men were well outnumbered since their clansmen had not yet arrived in from the surrounding countryside.

But, nothing daunted, they charged wildly into the fray, though at first the interlopers carried all before them.

The Maclaurins were driven back for a mile where reninforcements arrived and the Buchanans were surrounded and systematically massacred, only two of them escaping by swimming a cold, frothy river, though even this pair were hunted down and slain with a bloodthirsty efficiency typical of those warlike times.

Chapter four:

A disputed chieftainship

The Clan MacLaren chieftainship has long been a matter of controversy; and the attempt of the High Court Judge, John Maclaurin, Lord Dreghorn, in 1781 to establish his claim to honorary leadership was generally viewed as vain and flippant.

The official chieftainship actually fell into abeyance 500 years ago; and the last official record of its existence lies in the dusty scrolls of the clan listings drawn up in the late sixteenth century for King James VI who hit upon the novel notion that Highland leaders should be responsible for the behaviour of their followers.

In 1344, the last Celtic Earl of Strathearn was deprived of his title; and his lands and vassals eventually became vested in the Crown.

The Maclaurins thus found themselves reduced from the position of proprietors to that of tenants.

They appealed for protection to the powerful Campbell faction but the price was too high - the Lords of Argyll wanted the Maclaurins to bow down before them and recognise the Campbells as feudal superiors.

But the Maclaurins preferred giving their allegiance to the Crown; and successive kings recognised them in turn as an independent clan.

The first modern chieftain to be recognised by the Lord Lyon was MacLaren of Achleskine who purchased the ancient clan hunting grounds around the Boar's Rock.

He died in 1966 and was, suitably enough, buried with his ancestors in the Old Kirk of Balquhidder. His son inherited the title of Chieftain.

Among famous MacLarens (this being a modern derivation of the earlier MacLaurin) have been the inspiring, charismatic kirk ministers John and Colin MacLaurin. The former, born in 1693, was a famous preacher and controversialist, a leader of the Intrusionists in the Church of Scotland and the author of a celebrated collection of *Sermons and Essays* published in 1755.

His brother Colin, five years younger, was regarded as 'the one mathematician of the first rank trained in Britain during the eighteenth century'.

He was Professor of Mathematics successively at Aberdeen and Edinburgh Universities.

During the '45 Rebellion - and in contrast to most of his clan - he helped organise the defence of Edinburgh against the Jacobites and consequently had to flee and hide in the hills, an experience which broke his health and caused his death the following year.

It was his son, an advocate and senator of the College of Justice with the title Lord Dreghorn, who vainly (in every sense of the word) claimed the chieftainship of his clan in 1781.

Another stout clansman was Archibald MacLaren, soldier and dramatist (a strange combination), who joined the army in 1755 and fought against the Americans during their rebellion.

On returning home, understandably disillusioned with military life following Britain's humiliating defeat at the hands of the colonists, he joined a troupe of strolling players and was the author of a number of plays and 'dramatic pieces'. He also wrote a critically acclaimed treatise on 'the Irish problem'.

Ewen MacLaurin from Argyll was also on the British side during the American Revolution. He raised, at his own expense, a force known as the South Carolina Loyalists who played a prominent if eventually futile part in the hostilities.

Another military man was Colonel James MacLaren who led the Bengal Infantry in Imperial India.

Charles MacLaren established *The Scotsman* newspaper in 1817 and edited it from 1820 until 1845. He also found time to edit the *Encyclopedia Britannica* and published several important works on geology.

Gildwell in Essex is the principle training centre for British scout leaders and the Park there was gifted by William MacLaren in 1919; and in his memory any leader who has gained his Wood

Badge wears a patch of MacLaren tartan on his neckerchief. The North American Scouts have established a special membership and anyone with the Wood Badge may join.

The annual Lochearnhead Highland Games are usually held on the third Saturday of July. The MacLaren Clan always have a tent on these occasions and the clansmen are delighted to welcome their brethren and sisterhood from throughout the world as well as any interested visitors.

Lochearnhead, in the middle of scenic lands once fought over by clansmen protecting their territories at the point of their claymores, is now a renowned water sports centre; and there are several top class hotels in the district from where the past can be studied in comfort.

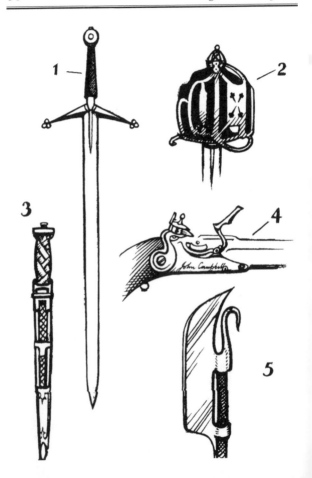

Highland weapons

1) The claymore or two-handed sword
   (fifteenth or early sixteenth century)

2) Basket hilt of broadsword
   made in Stirling, 1716

3) Highland dirk
   (eighteenth century)

4) Steel pistol *(detail)* made in Doune

5) Head of Lochaber Axe as carried
   in the '45 and earlier